To _____

Presented in God's Love
by   _____
St. Paul's United Methodist Church

....

....

....

More prayer resources at:
www.PrayersForOurLives.org

Also by Mel Lawrenz

How to Understand the Bible (WordWay, 2014)

Life After Grief (WordWay, 2015)

Overcoming Guilt and Shame (WordWay, 2015)

Spiritual Influence: The Hidden Power Behind Leadership (Zondervan, 2012)

I Want to Believe: Finding Your Way in An Age of Many Faiths (Regal, 2007)

Whole Church: Leading from Fragmentation to Engagement (Jossey-Bass/Leadership Network, 2009)

Patterns: Ways to Develop a God-Filled Life (Zondervan, 2003)

Putting the Pieces Back Together: How Real Life and Real Faith Connect (Zondervan, 2005)

For more resources:

www.WordWay.org
www.PrayersForOurLives.org
www.TheBrookNetwork.org
Facebook: thebrooknetwork
Twitter: MelLawrenz

Prayers for Our Lives

95 Lifelines to God for Everyday Circumstances

MEL LAWRENZ

WWW.WORDWAY.ORG

Mel writes with disarming honesty, and each prayer is like a cry of the heart. Here child-like simplicity meets sage-like wisdom, all of it spoken so intimately that living breath still seems to fill each word. Lifelines indeed.

—Mark Buchanan, author, pastor, and professor

Mel is a thoughtful analyst of church life today. Best of all—he actually does what he writes about.

—John Ortberg, author and pastor

Having known Mel Lawrenz for thirty-five years in various capacities as student, intern, colleague, and eventual successor as senior pastor of Elmbrook Church, I can testify to his keen mind, his profound respect for and knowledge of history, his forward-looking curiosity, his undoubted communication gifts, and his many years as a seasoned practitioner of church ministry.

—Stuart Briscoe, author and pastor

Mel Lawrenz's vision of a local church that actually reflects the wholeness and beauty of God as it engages with the Lord, one another, and the community is a much-needed call back to God's original Plan A – a plan that has too often been cast aside in the name of specialization, church growth, and expediency.

—Larry Osborne, author and pastor

CONTENTS

PART 3 - PRAYERS FOR STRESSFUL TIMES

PART 4 - PRAYERS FOR JOYOUS TIMES

PART 5 - PRAYERS FOR WORSHIPING GOD

PART 6 - PRAYERS FOR THE COMMUNITY, THE NATION, AND THE WORLD

PART 7 - PRAYERS FOR HOLIDAYS

PART 8 - PRAYERS FROM SCRIPTURE

PART 9 - ONE-SENTENCE PRAYERS

How to Use this Book of Prayers

I don't know about you, but sometimes I really need help in praying. I know how to pray. I know I can speak to God at any time in any place. But sometimes I benefit from prayers that have been written by others.

We all do this, of course, if we read the Psalms or the many prayers in the New Testament. We do it when we say the Lord's Prayer. We do this when we listen to someone else leading in prayer.

Of all the kinds of writing I get to do, one of the most satisfying is writing prayers that may benefit others. I love it when a church congregation joins its voice in prayer, and I'm glad when I can post a prayer that offers a lifeline to God someone may need.

This book of 95 prayers has nine sections:

- Prayers for Daily Patterns;
- Prayers for Difficult Times;
- Prayers for Stressful Times;
- Prayers for Joyous Times;
- Prayers for Worshiping God;
- Prayers for the Community, the Nation, and the World;
- Prayers for Holidays;

- Prayers from Scripture;
- One-sentence Prayers.

I hope you find in these "lifelines to God" some patterns of speaking to God that will be helpful. They may be helpful for you to pray just as they are, or as patterns for you to shape your own conversations with God. You may wish to adapt the prayers, writing your own words in the margins. If you are a church leader, some of the prayers may be helpful for public worship or for certain kinds of meetings or for a class. Tools are at www.PrayersForOurLives.org.

This book of "lifelines to God" may also be something you will want to gift to a friend in need, a newly-wed couple, a new graduate, someone who is ill or bereaved, someone needing the words to begin a relationship with God, or even a skeptic.

Of course none of this would matter if the Lord and Creator of the universe was not interested in hearing from us. But God is. We honor God when we speak to him. And our conversation with God changes us.

—Mel Lawrenz

"Pray continually" (1 Thessalonians 5:17).

—Part 1—

PRAYERS FOR DAILY PATTERNS

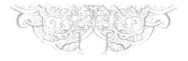

A Morning Prayer (A)

Dear Lord,

As this day begins I confess that I will need you every moment. I long to know you more deeply today. Help me in what I say to other people. Give me wisdom for each decision I will make. Make love and truth the motives behind everything I do. And when I fall short, help me not to give up, but to find an extra measure of your strength. This day is your creation and your gift. I commit my body and spirit to your good purposes.

In Jesus' name, Amen.

A Morning Prayer (B)

"Therefore I tell you, do not worry about your life, what you will eat or drink; or about your body, what you will wear. Is not life more than food, and the body more than clothes?... Therefore do not worry about tomorrow, for tomorrow will worry about itself. Each day has enough trouble of its own."

Matthew 6:25, 34

Dear Lord,

I admit that as this day begins I am filled with worry and trepidation. Life has been difficult lately. It makes me worry about what might happen today.

Help me to rest in the fact that not everything that could wrong today, will go wrong. Help me not to obsess about difficulties that haven't even happened yet.

Help me not to have undue worry about small things that do not matter in eternity.

And help me, most of all, to live in the riches of your love.

Amen.

A Morning Prayer (C)

Almighty God,

Thank you for the start of a new day. I am glad that, by your grace, I get to start again.

Yesterday is finished. Tomorrow has yet to come. But this day, today, is what is real right now. I know I may have to face difficulties, but I also know there are solutions I do not even know about yet.

Help me to walk by faith, and to please you in my thoughts, words, and deeds.

You have shown us, dear Lord, what is good, and what you require. "To act justly and to love mercy and to walk humbly"* with you.

With your help, I believe that can be my focus today.

In Christ's name. Amen.

An Evening Prayer (A)

Dear Lord,

As this day ends I am glad to be able to rest in you. I believe that you are with me and that you hear my prayer. May the good things that happened today be planted deeply in the memory of my heart and shape me into a better person. Help me to learn from my mistakes and sins. Thank you for the promise of a new beginning when I awake. Now allow me to rest in you and you alone, body, mind, heart, and spirit, to awake refreshed in the goodness of your care.

In Jesus' name, Amen.

---

* Micah 6:8

An Evening Prayer (B)

Dear Lord,

I am thinking about the good things and the challenging things that happened today. There is always so much of life that is outside of my control, and I don't always make the best choices with what I do control.

So once again, I am glad you allow me to live in a steady stream of your mercy. I would be completely lost without you.

I need rest now. So I commit my mind, body, and spirit to you. I rest in you.

In Jesus' name. Amen.

An Evening Prayer (C)

The day is done, dear Lord.

I commit my body to your healing.

I commit my mind to your instruction.

I commit my heart to your filling.

I commit my family to your care.

I release to you my anxieties and fears, my biases and prejudices, my hopes and aspirations.

I rest in you, Lord God Almighty.

Amen.

A Prayer to Start the Work Day

Lord, *I'm going to work now.*

It seems like it was just an hour ago I was waking up and getting ready to do my work. One day seems to run into the next. So I pray that today you would show me something new, teach me something new, and let me do something new that will be constructive, will help someone else, and will glorify you.

Lord, *I'm going to sweat now.*

It isn't like living in the Garden of Eden. But I know that in the field of this world[*] I can honor you in my work. I know that today I will face challenges and probably some frustrations. Help me know how to respond to any bad attitudes or influences I may encounter. Let me see how I can be a positive influence where I work. Sanctify my own attitude, raise me above my own fallen nature, empower me to uphold righteous values, and help me to persevere, especially when the work is hard.

Lord, *I'm going to serve now.*

---

[*] Genesis 3:17-19

Thank you for giving me the opportunity to be a blessing to someone else today in the work I do. You have created this world and everybody and everything in it. Help me see how I can bring your light and life to someone else today. Grant me wisdom to make good choices throughout the day. Prompt me to be compassionate toward the unemployed and the underemployed. I want to conduct myself according to the character of Jesus. And whatever I do, I want to do it in his name and for his sake.

Amen.

"And whatever you do, whether in word or deed, do it all in the name of the Lord Jesus, giving thanks to God the Father through him."

Colossians 3:17

When We Need Guidance

Dear God,

I desperately need your guidance at this time. Important decisions are before me, and they could affect other people and the course of my life.

Grant me faith in these decisions so that I can see the big picture, including your desires.

Grant me courage because I do not want to look only for the easy answers.

Grant me the wisdom from above that is "pure, peace-loving, considerate, submissive, full of mercy and good fruit, impartial, and sincere."*

Please help me find the right people whose counsel could be helpful.

As David "inquired of the Lord," again and again, I now make my inquiry of you, dear God. Protect me from my own subjectivity. Please develop a conviction in my heart that is consistent with your will and your ways. Guide me, I pray.

In Christ's name. Amen.

---

* James 3:17

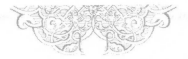

At Mealtime (A)

Lord Jesus, you taught us to pray, "give us this day our daily bread," and so now we thank you as we sit down to receive the blessings of this table. You make the grain and the nuts, the fruits and vegetables, the fish and the meat. We thank you for food that nourishes our bodies, and also that you, the "bread sent from heaven," nourish our souls as well.

Amen.

At Mealtime (B)

Bless us, O Lord, as we receive your gifts of food and drink which we receive out of your bountiful love.

Through Christ our Lord, Amen.

At Mealtime (C)

For the food we receive now, Lord, we give you thanks.

For the company we share around this table, Lord, we give you thanks.

For your presence in this moment, Lord God of Heaven, we give you thanks.

Amen.

Before and After Reading Scripture

Open my eyes, gracious Lord, as I turn to your word. I long to know you, to understand life, and to be changed. Examine me, Lord, by the floodlight of your truth.

Amen.

May the word I have read, Lord, be planted deeply in my mind and heart. Help me not to walk away and forget it,* but to meditate on it and obey it and so build my life on the rock of your truth.†

Amen.

---

* James 1:22-25

† Matthew 7:24

Asking God for Wisdom

"But the wisdom that comes from heaven is first of all pure;
then peace-loving, considerate, submissive, full of mercy
and good fruit, impartial and sincere."

James 3:17

Dear God, I need your higher wisdom. The wisdom of this world is not enough. It is not strong enough, it is not good enough, it is not steady enough.

The wisdom you give is "pure," dear God. You know my inner motives better than I do. You know my good motives, my bad motives, and my mixed motives. Purify me, that I may be wiser.

The wisdom you give is "peace-loving." Help me to cherish peace, to live in peace, and to be a peacemaker for others.

The wisdom you give is "considerate." Help me not to be selfish, unsympathetic, ungracious, impolite, or rude toward others, especially those I am closest to. Give me a caring spirit.

The wisdom you give is "submissive." I know I am sometimes stubborn and unyielding. Sometimes I think I know more than I do. Grant me a teachable spirit. Help me to cooperate with others rather than just trying to get my way.

The wisdom you give is "full of mercy and good fruit." Help me to have mercy toward others while still holding on to your truth. Guide me into acts of mercy that will be fruitful.

The wisdom you give is "impartial." Make me a fair-minded person, Lord. I admit I often act out of my own biases. Raise me above my preferences. Make me truthful and make me fair so that I can help others.

The wisdom you give is "sincere," gracious Lord. I admit to being hypocritical at times. I know I am not always honest in what I say. I regret that sometimes others don't trust me. I long for the freedom that comes from truthfulness.

Lord, help me find others who have "the wisdom that comes from heaven," and to learn from them. And may others find that in me.

Amen.

For Our Families

"For this reason I kneel before the Father, from whom every family in heaven and on earth derives its name."

Ephesians 3:14-15

Dear heavenly Father,

I pray for my family.

I pray for our children who need your protection and whose hearts and minds are developing every day in ways hidden from our eyes. Help us to live in grace and truth so that our influence in their lives will provide them with mercy and righteousness. Protect them at school, at home, on the playground, and when they are with friends. Help our children to know of your fatherly care.

We need help in our marriages, O God. Help us to have respect for each other and love that inspires us to serve one another. May we forbear each others' minor faults, and forgive each other our sins. Help us to understand each other. Help us to be honest. Give us patience and hope.

We pray for all the families in our communities and in our nation. We are grieved that the ideal of the family is long-forgotten in so many places. Our families need to be revived, dear God. May it begin with us.

Amen.

When We Travel

Lord, as I prepare to travel I ask you for protection and guidance.

I know you are with me wherever I go. Knowing you as Lord Almighty over all creation comforts me. There is not any place on earth that you do not claim as your own. I am always under your sovereign hand.

You command your people to go, to move, to journey, and you show yourself as the journey master.

Reassure my loved ones when I am not with them. Grant your travel mercies when I am in a car, plane, train, or bus. Help me to represent you well with whomever I have contact.

In Jesus' name. Amen.

—Part 2—

PRAYERS FOR DIFFICULT TIMES

When Someone Is Ill

Dear God,

I am watching someone I love suffer in illness. This is so hard for me to witness. I wish I could do something to take the pain and distress away. I feel so helpless.

I'm not sure what to say and what not to say, so I need your guidance and wisdom. Help me to remain faithful and patient. Help me to think more of _____ than myself. Remove from me any hint of resentment I may have.

Please reach into this situation with your restorative touch. Work in the hidden parts of the body. Help everyone to find connections with good physicians and other health care professionals. Please let _____ have a sense of you as the Great Physician.

Please, dear God, bring to _____ a sense of your loving presence. Help loved ones to know that, too.

We know we do not know the future, but I pray that you help us to see that you hold the future.

Thank you, Lord Jesus, for suffering on our behalf. We need you, great Shepherd of the sheep, to lead us all through the valley of illness.

In Christ's Name, Amen.

When We Are Ill

Dear God,

I hurt.

My body is not working like it used to. I do not like being weak. I do not like pain. I do not like uncertainty. Thank you for letting me tell you this.

Your word tells me that I can ask you for your healing. So I do ask you now. I plead with you now. Please make me more well than I am now.

My spirit groans within me, dear God. Because my body hurts, my soul hurts. I am discouraged. I need you to strengthen my heart. I do not want the suffering in my soul to affect my family and friends.

Help me, dear Lord, when people say things that do more harm than good. They may not know I do not need platitudes right now. I need them.

Dear God, my hurting body causes me to feel so alone. I don't want to be limited. I don't want to be confined to my bed. I feel ashamed that I am not able to accomplish what I used to. I hate feeling like I'm letting other people down.

Help me, dear God, not to listen to false promises. But help me also not to be hopeless.

I look to you, Lord Jesus, my suffering savior, my hurting Lord, my rejected friend. As you looked beyond the cross, scorning its shame, and had joy for what lay ahead, give me faith to have a settled soul, whatever is in my path.

Amen.

When a Loved One Has Died

Dear God,

That final moment has come. I know that we all die, but the finality of the death is hitting us very hard.

I am thinking of people whose lives will have to adjust to this loss. I want to believe that they will be able to carry on, even if it seems so difficult. I beg you to come alongside those who are grieving the most. Help them to honor their loved one who has passed. Help them to hang on for the season of mourning that lies ahead.

Your word says that "it is better to go to a house of mourning," and that "a sad face is good for the heart."* This is challenging to believe, but we know we would not be grieving if not for the fact that the life of our loved one was a blessing you gave to all of us.

So help us to hold on to hope, to have deep faith, and to appreciate love, in this difficult time.

In Christ's name, Amen.

---

* Ecclesiastes 7:2-3

"And now these three remain: faith, hope and love. But the greatest of these is love."

1 Corinthians 13:13

When We Face Unemployment

Lord God,

I did not plan on being unemployed at this time, and it has put me in a difficult place.

Help me to have faith when I am afraid. I do not know what will happen if this goes on for too long.

Help me when I feel embarrassed about my situation. I know there are reasons why I am not to blame, but I wrestle every day with what might have been if I had made different choices. This is not helping my situation, so please help me to get over shame that stands in my way. I want to be able to tell people my situation just simply and honestly.

Even in this situation I take it by faith that you have good intentions for my life. Right now I don't even know what path my life will take. I know that everyone has to take a step of faith to believe in your sovereignty over all things. Help me to take that step every day.

Help me, Lord, to get over any pride that is holding me back. I want to have the courage to take any reasonable job, and to be glad that I am able to put food on the table.

I know, Lord, that there are things I probably need to learn during this period in my life. My mind and heart are open. Help me to learn today what I need to learn about myself and about life.

If there is someone I need to meet, a connection to make, a conversation to have, I humbly ask you to guide me to that person or those people. Help me to keep my eyes open, and prompt my friends to keep their eyes open, too.

Most of all, Lord, help me to persevere. Sometimes I really feel like giving up. I'm tired of disappointment. I'm tired of rejection. I'm tired of uncertainly. I know I will need your supernatural power to keep going. Help me to put one foot in front of the other, to persevere like all the great heroes of the faith.

In Christ's name, Amen.

"Now faith is confidence in what we hope for and assurance about what we do not see."

Hebrews 11:1

When We Are Lonely

Father God,

I speak to you now because it seems like there is no one else. Even when I am around other people, it feels like I'm floating past them, like they do not notice me, like they could care less if I exist or not.

I am tired of being so lonely.

I am tired of people being so wrapped up in themselves. I am tired of people spending so much energy trying to impress other people. I am tired of people being merely polite.

I do not know how things got to this point, dear Lord, but it has gone on a long time. I know that in life most people go through loneliness at one time or another. I do not want to become bitter, I just want things to improve.

I need your guidance. If I need to get into new situations, new communities, a new church, please give me the courage to do what is wise. If I have missed the clues that someone was trying to reach out to me and I did not reciprocate, please give me another chance. If I have been projecting a bad attitude or uncivil behavior, I am willing to change. But I need insight. And I need faith.

I am glad I can pray to you. Even when I have doubts that you are listening, I still know that it is right for me to pour out my heart to you. None of us has any right to presume upon your love and care. Yet you have told us all that you would be with us in every circumstance. That you will never abandon us. That you are there even when it seems no one else is.

I do rest in you today, Father.

Amen.

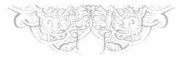

When We Are Depressed

Dear God,

I have come to a dark place. This has been developing for a long time. No one understands what is going on in me right now. Even I don't understand it fully.

Why do I have to suffer with this? Why is nothing making me feel any better? Why do I not sense any love or hope?

It is hard for me to remember when I did not feel this way. People tell me there is hope. I want to believe that, but it is difficult. My prayer to you is my call for help. Dear God, help me to know I have not been abandoned.

I am ashamed that I feel this way. I'm embarrassed that I am not able to be the person other people want me to be. But I know that all that matters is who I am in your sight. I know I have your grace and forgiveness. And I admit that I am a sinner, too.

I pray as did David "restore to me the joy of my salvation and grant me a willing spirit, to sustain me."

"Let me hear joy and gladness." Let my crushed bones rejoice.*

Let me hear the gentle whisper of your voice as did Elijah when he was alone and despondent.†

Lord Jesus, you said, "come to me, all you who are weary and burdened, and I will give you rest."‡ That sounds very good.

On this day I make this decision: I rest in you.

Amen.

---

* Psalm 51

† 1 Kings 19:12

‡ Matthew 11:28

When We Have Done Wrong

Dear God,

I confess to you, with open mind and heart, that I have sinned. You know the circumstances already. You know the wrongness of what I have done. You know—better than I do—why this happened.

I do not know why I made the choices I did. I sense the words of the apostle Paul: "I do not do the good I want to do, but the evil I do not want to do—this I keep on doing." And "although I want to do good, evil is right there with me."*

I am ashamed for what has happened. And so I pray: "God, have mercy on me, a sinner."† "I confess my iniquity; I am troubled by my sin."‡ "Wash away all my iniquity and cleanse me from my sin."§

I also confess my faith in Jesus. Today I focus on his suffering on the cross as the time when my sins

---

* Romans 7:19, 21

† Luke 18:13

‡ Psalm 38:18

§ Psalm 51:2

were laid on him. This overwhelms me. It humbles me.

Lord God, I know that this prayer is not enough on its own. I will need your protection when I am tempted. Help me to keep my focus on you every hour of every day. Break me out of cycles of the same sins.

In Christ's name, Amen.

When Visiting Someone in the Hospital

Dear Lord,

I pray for _____ right now.

Please help _____ with the long hours and inconvenience of being here.

Please guide the medical staff and doctors to provide good care and to know exactly what the problems are.

Bring healing, dear Lord.

Bring comfort.

Bring love.

We entrust _____ to your care, O Sovereign Lord, and will continue to do so every day.

In the name of Jesus, the Great Physician, Amen.

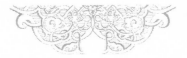

When a Friend Is Grieving

Dear Lord,

My heart is breaking for _____.
The loss is so great. The pain is so much. The loneliness is so deep.

I want to be able to help, but I feel helpless. Please give me wisdom to know what I might do to that shows my love and support.

Help me to see when I should be with _____, and when to stay away.

I want to be able to say things that will help, but I am afraid of saying the wrong thing. Please give me the right words at the right time. And help me to know when I should say very little.

I ask, dear Lord, for your mercy for my friend. Please help _____ to know your comfort and your love at this time.

In Christ's name, Amen.

—Part 3—

PRAYERS FOR STRESSFUL TIMES

When We Are Discouraged

Lord, I am discouraged today.

I had hoped the problems I am encountering would begin to get resolved a long time ago.

I had hoped I would know exactly what I could do to make things better.

I had hoped that other people would see that they are causing problems.

I had hoped that I could be a better person than I am.

I had hoped I could at least have a glimmer of hope.

I feel like I'm holding on by a thread. Some days it seems like I'm walking on the edge of a cliff. I know this is not good. I know it is not safe.

So today, dear God, I just ask you to help me hang in there. I intend to walk in faith today, but I may need extra help.

You are a God of great goodness. I do thank you for your great acts and your mercies in the past. I know that when all else seems disappointing, and when I am deeply discouraged by the people around me, you remain faithful. Your goodness and greatness will never change.

Help me to hold on to you.

Amen.

When We Are Angry

O God, I am so deeply troubled.

I am angry at someone right now, and I don't know what to do with it.

I think it's understandable that I am angry, but I'm not sure. I worry that this is wrong. I don't want to make a bad situation worse.

I ask you to help me with my anger. Either lessen the agitation of my heart, or help me to know what to do with it.

I do not know if it is right to say something right now. It may make things worse. Or my silence may make things worse. My anger tells me that something needs to change.

Maybe I need to change. If so, give me the courage to do that. But I don't want to take blame on my shoulders where I am innocent.

If I am indignant about something truly wrong, help me to stand up for that principle. But if I am angry for lesser reasons—because of my wounded ego, because I've lost something, because I'm just afraid—please help me to release my grip.

Help me to behave well as the fire slowly dies down. Prevent me from hurting others in my anger. And help me to walk in integrity.

In Christ's name, Amen.

When Facing Financial Difficulties

Dear Lord,

I really wish I did not have to pray right now about financial distress in my life. I wrestle with shame about it. I obsess about what is going to happen. I have a lot of fear.

Help me not to deal with this by denying the problems, Lord. I do not want to make things worse.

Help me to swallow hard and admit to you and to myself, and to my loved ones affected, what the situation is.

I know there are many people who have been where I am today, and have survived. Give me faith that my story can be similar.

Look into my heart, O God.

Cut out any attitude of entitlement or selfishness or greed that I have had.

Extinguish any shame that has caused me to use money as a way to feel good about myself.

Give me wisdom in financial matters, dear God.

Help me to work diligently and smartly.

Help me to have realistic expectations.

Help me to be generous even when I feel needy.

Help me to find reliable counselors who can give me steps toward financial freedom.

Help me to work well with other family members and come up with healthy mutual plans.

Help me to serve you, and not serve money.

Most of all, O God, help me to be patient, diligent, and faithful. Prevent me from looking for quick fixes. Protect me from people who would want to capitalize on my misfortune.

I trust you today, in Jesus' name, Amen.

When We Are Tempted

Lord God,

I am on shaky ground right now because I am being strongly tempted.

It took me a while to see what was happening on the outside, and what is happening within me—in my mind and heart. I did not even want to pray about this because I was fooling myself into thinking this was not a big deal. And then I naively thought that I could deal with the temptation on my own.

This is dangerous, and so I pray to you now. I pray with urgency. Help me to step back from the edge of this cliff. Show me how I can separate myself from the opportunity to sin. Shout at me if I am standing too close to the edge.

I know I should talk to someone else about what is happening, but I am hesitant. I don't want anyone to think ill of me. I don't want to alarm those who love me. I don't want to lose something unnecessarily.

Give me the courage to talk to a trusted spiritual confidant, and with other people in my situation.

I now know, Lord Jesus, why you taught us to pray: "Lead us not into temptation." And "deliver us from the evil one."*

It is good that I am afraid when I realize I am being tempted. May all the choices I make today please you and set me on a path of security.

In Christ's name, Amen.

---

* Matthew 6:13

When We Are Confused

Dear Lord,

I am confused. I do not understand why people do what they do sometimes.

"I do not understand what I do. For what I want to do I do not do, but what I hate I do."*

Why do things happen that just don't make sense? Why do some problems just never go away? Why do people keep making the same mistakes?

Lord, your patience is great. It is amazing that you have not given up on the human race. I am grateful for your forbearance. It comforts me.

There is so much misunderstanding in our world.

So much bias.

So much prejudice.

So much one-sided thinking.

May clarity begin with me, dear God. I long to be a wise person. Clear up my confusion so that I may make good decisions. And help me to help others when they feel confused.

Amen.

---

* Romans 7:15

PRAYERS FOR OUR LIVES

—Part 4—

PRAYERS FOR JOYOUS TIMES

A Prayer of Faith and Salvation

O God,

I now know that I want my life to be fully in your hands. This is right. It is time for me to hold back no longer.

You have brought me to this place. I know I am not merely imagining that you are real, and I am not just following what my friends and family want.

And so I confess to you that I am a sinner. I have sinned in my thoughts, and in my words, and in my deeds. Sometimes I sinned intentionally, and oftentimes by mistake. I want you to be the master of my life, not sin.

I confess that I believe in Jesus Christ. Though I have much to learn, I understand Jesus came to save us from our sins. His life was perfect, and in his death on the cross he offered forgiveness. He is Lord of all.

I humbly accept your great gift of mercy. You have done this, great God.

Heavenly Father, I want to live under your care every day.

Lord Jesus, it is right for me to follow you.

Holy Spirit, I am empty unless you fill me, broken unless you heal me, weak unless you empower me.

I am uncertain of what will happen next in my life, so help me, dear God, to have faith every day. Bring people into my life who can teach me what life in Jesus can be. I throw myself on your mercy today.

I pray this prayer with faith in you and in your amazing grace.

Amen.

On Friendship

Dear Lord,

Thank you for the friends you have brought into my life. I know we have our ups and downs, and some friends have come and gone. Sometimes I am disappointed that my friends do not understand me more fully, but I also know that I have disappointed them.

Help me to keep things simple. I am glad for the people I can call, for the people who do care.

This makes me think of the people I know who have no real friends. My heart goes out to them. My heart breaks for them when I see how lonely they are sometimes.

Help me to be a friend to the friendless. I know I cannot rescue other people, but I know I can love them. Help me to have the courage and generosity to say something or do something of grace when I have the chance. And help them to come to find you as their truest friend.

In Christ, Amen.

Thanks for Good Health

Dear Lord,

I want to thank you for the good health I enjoy at this time. Our bodies are so complex, it is amazing that they work at all. I am amazed at your handiwork in creating our bodies.

Show me disciplines that will help me to stay healthy. I know I should respect my body as a temple of the Holy Spirit. This is amazing. I want to be as strong and healthy as I can be, not just for my sake, but so that I may be able to serve others well.

In Christ's name, Amen.

Thanks for Successful Medical Treatment

Dear Lord,

Thank you that I was able to get good medical treatment. I do not take this for granted.

The work of healing lies ahead, and so I ask you for patience day by day. I praise you for the amazing process of healing you do in our bodies every day. You really are the Great Physician.

Help me to cooperate with the treatment process. I am grateful for the medical resources I was able to find.

I know that every one of us, every single day, must walk in faith. We are "fearfully and wonderfully made,"* but we are also vulnerable and fallible. I want to praise you when I am weak and when I am strong.

In Jesus' name, Amen.

---

* Psalm 139:14

Thanks for an Ordinary Day

Lord God, today was a simple, ordinary day. I am grateful for it.

There was a time when I would have called this kind of day boring or routine or uninteresting. But I choose to see your work in the ordinary moments in my life.

I had food on the table today. Thank you.

I was able to do my work today. Thank you.

I took care of personal and family needs today. Thank you.

I had the opportunity to look for insight from you today. Thank you.

I had respectful conversations today. Thank you.

I long to see your lordship every day, dear Lord—on days when you do extraordinary things, and on days when you allow our lives to glorify you in simple, quiet ways.

In Christ's name, Amen.

Gratitude for a Major Achievement

Lord God, this is a day to celebrate. I am so deeply grateful that diligent work and effort has led to this major achievement.

I know that you deserve not just thanks, but praise as well. I can do nothing without you. In your wisdom you created us all with energy and drive, with a longing to succeed and to excel. You give us the opportunity to improve our lives and the lives of the people around us.

So I am glad for the congratulations that have come my way for this achievement, but I praise you, great God of heaven and earth, for your ongoing work among us.

Lead us on to the challenges and opportunities that lay before us.

In Christ's name, Amen.

When a New Baby Arrives

Dear Lord,

We thank you and praise you for the arrival of this new life. We are amazed and awestruck at the wonder of this new birth. After months of waiting, we now can see and know this new creation.

Your word tells us that you knit us together in our mothers' wombs, that we are fearfully and wonderfully made, that you saw our unformed bodies, and that all the days ordained for us are written in your book.*

And so we pray now for this little one. We pray for health and well being. We pray for this child's parents. Give them wisdom and strength for these new days, and also for years to come as they care for their child in obedience to you.

In the name of Jesus. Amen.

---

* Psalm 139:16

For Graduation

Dear Lord,

We are so glad to celebrate the graduation of
_____. This is a major achievement. We
are grateful. Thank you for this milestone.

We ask for your guidance and protection at this
turning point and new beginning.

We ask for an abundance of wisdom for
_____ as important decisions come
up.

You are Lord of heaven and earth. We trust in
your providential care.

In Christ's name. Amen.

When Someone Comes to Faith

Lord God, how glad we are that our friend has come to faith in you!

Your word tells us that the angels rejoice, that you are are glad, and so we are thrilled that new spiritual life has begun.

Like the father in the story of the prodigal son, we see you welcoming a child back home. It reminds us of the joy of our salvation, the peace that comes from finding our way to you.

We pray for protection from the evil one. We know that evil does not want new spiritual life, and will seek to ruin it.

We pray for a path forward for our friend—for good fellowship, good learning from sound teaching, and wisdom as life's issues come up in whole new ways.

We stand amazed at your invisible, mysterious work, Holy Spirit, by which our friend has come to faith.

In Christ's name. Amen.

When Someone Gets Married

Lord God, we celebrate the marriage of
_____ and _____.

We know marriage is an honorable institution which you ordained at the beginning. It is the building block of society, the foundation of the family, and a relationship that mirrors the relationship of Christ and the church.

So on this day we consider marriage with all the seriousness it deserves. We ask your blessing on _____ and _____ in the years to come.

Protect them in a relationship of mutual respect.

Bless them with shared love.

Guide them in decisions large and small.

Keep them humble and forgiving.

Teach them forbearance.

Strengthen them when they face challenges.

Speak to them when problems are still small.

Lead them into a reverence for you.

And grant them the gift of mutual joy both today, and in the days to come.

In the name of Jesus. Amen.

PRAYERS FOR OUR LIVES

Part 5

PRAYERS FOR
WORSHIPING GOD

Praise to God the Father

Holy Father in heaven, how grateful we are for your great power and providence. You are not like the phantom gods which human beings have fabricated. You are the one and only true God, not a lie.

O Father, you are great and you are good.

Great because you are Spirit.

Great because you exist before all things.

Great because you are the living God and are the author of life.

Great because you are the personal God, the God of Abraham, of Isaac, and of Jacob

—not the God of empty philosophy.

Great because you know all things.

Great because you are Almighty.

Great because you are present everywhere.

Great because you do not change.

Father, you are great, and you are good. Else we would be in danger.

Good because you are holy.

Good because you are righteous.

Good because you are just.

Good because you are love.

Good because you are truth.

Your greatness and goodness, O Father, exceed our comprehension. But any day we catch a glimmer of your glory, our lives are better.

We have been prodigals,* Father. We want to come home. We want to stay at home.

Amen.

---

* Luke 15

Praise to Christ the Lord

Lord Jesus Christ, we adore you and praise you. Where would we be without you? We long to live in your glory and your goodness.

You identified yourself with God the Father when you said "I am." You explained your life and purpose by saying...

"I am the bread of life"*—and so we know we live through you.

"I am the light of the world"—and so we no longer live in the darkness of evil and ignorance.

"I am the gate for the sheep"—and so we know we are protected from spiritual predators.

"I am the good shepherd"—and so we are well fed, and led, and protected.

"I am the resurrection and the life"—and so we can live above the fear of illness and death.

"I am the way, the truth, and the life"—and so we see a clear way forward toward abundant life.

---

*The 7 "I am" passages are John 6:35-51; 8:12; 10:9; 10:11-14; 11:25; 14:6; 15:1-5.

80

"I am the true vine"—and so we know staying connected to you is the most important priority we must have.

Lord Jesus, you are "the author of life."* You came so that we may have life, and have it to the full.†

We can stand before God the Father because of your great sacrifice. You made peace through the blood of your cross, in order to reconcile all things to yourself.‡

We are overwhelmed. We are in awe. We are humbled. We wish to worship and follow you all the days of our lives. We want to know you—yes, to know the power of your resurrection and participation in your sufferings, becoming like you in your death, and so, somehow, attaining to the resurrection from the dead.§

Amen.

---

* Acts 3:15

† John 10:10

‡ Colossians 1:20

§ Philippians 3:10-11

Praise to the Holy Spirit[*]

Come, Holy Spirit, come.

Since you came as the "advocate" Jesus spoke about, the world has never been the same. And so we ask now:

Fill us with your awe-inspiring glory.

Empower us for the great mission to which we are called.

Pour out your love and your gifts.

Enlighten us with the truth of the word of God.

Grant us the righteousness, peace, and joy that your presence brings.

Purify us through your sanctifying work.

Protect us, Holy Spirit, so that we do not grieve you, or quench you, or resist you.

We want to keep in step with you, Holy Spirit. We need a lifelong fellowship with you. May our lives show the fruit of your presence, transforming us into

---

* Scripture allusions in this prayer: John 14:16; Ephesians 5:18; Romans 15:13; 5:5; 17:14; Ephesians 4:30; 1 Thessalonians 5:19; Acts 7:51; Galatians 5:25; 2 Corinthians 13:14; Galatians 5:22-23.

people of love, joy, peace, patience, kindness, goodness, faithfulness, gentleness, and self control.

Come, Holy Spirit, come.

A Prayer of Dedication in Church

Heavenly Father, you are good to us. Your mercy is everlasting. For all our faults you still call your church your bride. Help us to honor you. Help us to represent you to our community and our world in ways that show your grace and truth. By your greatness make us greater in thought, word, and deed.

Jesus, everything is different because you came. You have made us free. You have healed. You redeem and reconcile. Help us to stand for what you stand for. Break the bondage of sin in our lives. Bring reconciliation to broken relationships. Make us bold witnesses for you. Motivate us to assist the poor and the oppressed. Help us to proclaim the year of your favor.*

Holy Spirit, your work is mighty. Your ways are mysterious. Fill, us, we pray. Guide us, comfort us, teach us. May we not grieve you or quench your work among us. Keep our hearts open.

Dear God, we want to be a church that gives glory to you—Father, Son, and Holy Spirit. We com-

---

* Luke 4:19

84

mit ourselves to worship and serve you. Your call and your mission is our life.

In Christ's name, Amen.

At a Funeral

We come to you, dear God, at this time of loss, because it is better for us to mourn before you than to mourn alone.

Thank you for what you did in and through the life of our loved one.

Thank you that nothing can take away our living memories.

Thank you that there is hope on the other side of this life—where you wipe every tear from our eyes and where there is no more death or mourning or crying or pain.*

Please comfort everyone, especially our closest family and friends.

Help us to look at our lives differently.

Help us to cherish every hour.

Help us to long to live on a higher plane and to seek integrity in our lives.

Help us to be unsatisfied with our own misbehavior.

Help us to forgive.

---

* Revelation 21:4

Help us to love.

Help us to hope.

Help us to see Jesus Christ, alive and victorious, holding his outstretched hand in front of us.

Help us to see light ahead and not darkness so that we will be children of light and so glorify you.

In the name of the crucified and risen Christ,

Amen.

—Part 6—

PRAYERS FOR THE COMMUNITY, THE NATION, AND THE WORLD

For the Community

Dear God,

We pray for our community.

We begin by thanking you for your rich blessings. We thank you for the care and purpose with which you created the heavens and the earth. Thank you that we can see the splendor of your creation. We see the majesty of your character in what you have made: the streams and hills, the lakes and forests, in fields that bear rich harvests.

We thank you for your influence in our culture and heritage. Help us to cling to values that stretch well beyond ourselves and the brief time we spend in this world.

We confess to you that our response to your goodness is often muted because we get entangled in things that are temporary and passing away.

We ask for your forgiveness and your mercy, and ask that you would drive us to faith and direct our vision to building our lives and communities with truth and integrity.

We pray now that you would help every person who has a role in governing our community and nation to understand the value you place on what they do. Help each one to sense the satisfaction that comes from being a public servant.

We pray specifically for matters of great weight that must be dealt with in these days: matters of public security and of social justice and of fiscal management. As the Bible invites us to ask you for wisdom whenever we need it—we do ask on behalf of every person making decisions that affect the lives of many, that you would give a wisdom that is deep and selfless and true.

We thank you that you hear our prayers, and long to hear prayers both made in public and voiced in the quiet corners of our lives. And so we pray for your providential care and protection over our community.

Amen.

For the Nation (A)

Dear God,

You have said in your word that whenever we know we need wisdom, we should ask for it, and that you will give it generously.* As we take the extraordinary step to vote for our local, regional, and national leaders, we pray for your wisdom from above.

Grant us wisdom to know the way you look on the affairs of our nation.

Grant us wisdom to understand how you view our world today.

Grant us wisdom to know what an ordered and just and compassionate society looks like.

Grant us wisdom to know what to do with the reality of evil.

Grant us wisdom to uphold the defenseless.

Grant us wisdom to love you and love our neighbor as ourselves.

Lord, we pray that our leaders will personally understand that you are a dynamic reality in the world and in our lives.

---

* James 1:5

May we be a nation which depends on you, acknowledges your blessings, and values what you value.

And on the day after the election, Lord, help us to be faithful members of your kingdom and responsible citizens of the nation we inhabit.

In Christ's name and for his sake, Amen.

For the Nation (B)

Dear God,

You have blessed us with the gift of life, and so, with every breath we take, we are your testimony of the value and sanctity of life. You have blessed us by putting us in a world that is your spectacular creation full of wonder; and you allow us to live in a nation rich with natural resources and incredible beauty. Help us to marvel at the blessings of your creation and to be responsible stewards of the land you have made.

You have blessed us with marriage and family and friendship. And so we ask you to help us cherish and respect these relationships you have woven into the human race, and may we honor those relationships by living them out with grace and truth.

You have blessed us with the gift of freedom.

The freedom by which we can gather together.

The freedom by which we make sober choices about how we conduct ourselves as a nation.

The freedom by which we can show acts of mercy to those who suffer or are disadvantaged.

The freedom by which we as citizens may exercise responsible discernment in the selection of our leaders.

The freedom by which we as fathers and mothers, sisters and brothers, and friends and neighbors and fellow-workers can build each other up to be the people you created us to be.

We pray for the leaders of our nation. Please bless and empower and guide them in these days which are the stepping stones to our future.

We acknowledge our daily need for your forgiveness of our shortcomings, and acknowledge our need for your protection against those who would harm and destroy. We are citizens of this nation, but we know that, to you, all the nations are together like a drop in a bucket, as dust on the scales.[*]

We are today and always under your watchful eye as loving Father, saving Son, and purifying Holy Spirit.

Amen.

---

[*] Isaiah 40:12-15

For the World

Do you not know?

Have you not heard?

Has it not been told you from the beginning?

Have you not understood since the earth was founded?

He sits enthroned above the circle of the earth,

and its people are like grasshoppers.

He stretches out the heavens like a canopy,

and spreads them out like a tent to live in.

He brings princes to naught

and reduces the rulers of this world to nothing.

Isaiah 40:21-23

Great Lord of heaven and earth,

We pray for our world.

But it is not *our* world, of course, it is *your* world. By your sovereign choice you created the heavens and the earth. Your power and beauty are everywhere to be seen in the creation. You chose to make humanity according to your image.

But we men and women have chosen to follow our own ways. We separated ourselves from you. We ruined the world.

We rejoice that you so loved the world, that you have come in the person of Jesus Christ to save us.

And so we pray for the process of salvation in our world.

Help us to see your light even when darkness seems to surround us.

Help us to proclaim Jesus Christ, the light that has come into the world, at every opportunity.

Grant freedom so we may proclaim the gospel without impediment.

Help those whose very lives are threatened in persecution.

Bring your holy judgment against all evil.

Let your justice roll on like a river.[*]

Bring peace to troubled regions of the world.

Guide us into the ways we can be peacemakers, as the Lord Jesus commanded.[†]

Give us the courage to be peacemakers when others only want conflict and war.

Build in us an integrity of attitude, behavior, and character that will let the world know that we can return to your goodness.

In the powerful name of Jesus, Amen.

---

[*] Amos 5:24

[†] Matthew 5:9

For the Poor and the Downtrodden

"The Spirit of the Lord is on me,
because he has anointed me
to proclaim good news to the poor.
He has sent me to proclaim freedom for the prisoners
and recovery of sight for the blind,
to set the oppressed free,
to proclaim the year of the Lord's favor."

Luke 4:18-19

Gracious Lord in heaven,

When we consider the misery and suffering of so many millions of people in the world today, we are overwhelmed.

May we not turn away.

Help us to see these realities. Open our ears to the cries of the multitudes. Give us the courage to know the pain of others.

And so we pray, though with a great sense of our limitations.

We pray for the poor. May the battle against extreme poverty go on without pause.

We pray for the oppressed. Help them to survive the corruptions of governments and the evil of criminals who prey on them.

We pray for the enslaved. Bring them rescuers who will break them out of their bondage. Give them hope for spiritual freedom.

We pray for those who suffer the indignity of discrimination in any form. Help them find justice, and protect their hearts from bitterness.

We pray for the courageous people who are bringing release and relief to the poor and downtrodden in our world. We pray they would have resources to do the job and that they would sense your wisdom to know what may be done.

We are overwhelmed by the needs of a suffering world, dear God. Protect us from paralysis. Help us to proclaim the liberating gospel of the Lord Jesus, and to live out that gospel.

In Christ's name, Amen.

For Leaders in Government

Dear God,

We will perish in foolishness if we do not grow in wisdom. We need leaders who, like Solomon, look to you for wisdom.

We pray for all our leaders in government. We pray for local leaders, including our advocates and judges and law enforcement officers. We pray for regional and state leaders, for governors and agency heads. We pray for our national leaders, including members of Congress and the President.

Help them to be servants of the common good and to see that temptations to personal power are deadly. Help them to find truth-telling more satisfying than lying. Help them to see their authority as a God-given responsibility, rather than personal privilege.

Give them wisdom, dear God. Motivate them to act rationally and for the common good. Inspire them to behave with respect and dignity.

Lessen the foolishness of simple-mindedness, the foolishness of carelessness, and the foolishness of cynicism.

We pray this in the name of the Messiah of whom Isaiah said: "the government will be on his shoulders."*

Amen.

---

* Isaiah 9:6

—Part 7—

PRAYERS FOR HOLIDAYS

For Thanksgiving Day

"Do not be anxious about anything, but in every situation, by prayer and petition, with thanksgiving, present your requests to God."

Philippians 4:6

Dear God,

You have invited us to give you thanks, and this is what we wish to do. We are living in a time of great anxiety, but you have offered us a way out of anxiety. We long to know your loving care.

We pray to you because there is no one so good, so high, so holy, and so merciful as you. Thank you that you have invited us to bring our petitions and our requests to you. Who else can we go to for wisdom, or for hope, or for guidance?

We pray for the victims of violence wherever they may be found. We pray for those in authority, that they would seek and find the wisdom that comes from above. We pray for peace in the world.

We pray that you would help us live in obedience, with integrity, based on the dignity you have given. And we pray for peace in our own hearts, a peace that proceeds from your forgiveness, the wholeness that comes from your restorative touch.

We thank you for creating a world you called "good." We thank you that despite the evil that has entered the world and still wages war in our own souls, your own goodness is undiminished. We thank you that we have seen

honor that is bolder than shame;

mercy that is wider than cruelty;

truth that is straighter than deception;

faith that is stronger than treachery;

hope that is deeper than desperation.

We thank you for the ordinary things: the bread we receive today, the breath by which we live today. And we thank you for the extraordinary things: the strength we didn't know was possible, and the discovery of truths we didn't know we didn't know. We thank you for the immeasurable grace shown to us in the coming of Jesus Christ, the hope of the world.

In his name, Amen.

For Advent and the Christmas Season

Lord God,

In these weeks leading up to Christmas we long to know the meaning, the power, and the mystery of that great mission whereby you came to save us from our sins.

Help us focus on the good news that has caused great joy for people around the world and across the ages.

We are in awe that the coming of the Lord Jesus has shaped the history of the world and has changed untold millions of lives. We need this gospel in troubled times lest we become cynical, doubtful, fearful, or vengeful. Strengthen our faith during challenging times.

We rejoice in the proclamation of Immanuel, God with us. As Isaiah said, "to us a child is born, to us a son is given, and the government will be on his shoulders. And he will be called Wonderful Counselor, Mighty God, Everlasting Father, Prince of Peace."*

We need the governing of the Lord Christ because humanity is so out of control.

We need the "Wonderful Counselor" because we wander in ignorance and foolishness so much of the time.

We need the savior who is "Mighty God," able to save and preserve.

We need an "Everlasting Father" who protects us and provides not what we think we need but what we truly need.

We need the "Prince of Peace" because of the tensions between the nations of the world, because there are thousands of people whose hearts are dark with thoughts of murder and terrorism, and because even friends and family members so often battle with each other.

We have always needed a savior. Now more than ever.

In the name of the Jesus the Christ, Son of God, Savior. Amen.

---

* Isaiah 9:6

For Christmas Day

Lord God,

"My eyes have seen your salvation, which you have prepared in the sight of all nations: a light for revelation to the Gentiles, and the glory of your people Israel."[*]

We rejoice in the coming of our Lord Jesus, the light of the world, who has pierced the darkness. He has come from you, O Father, full of your glory, full of grace and truth.[†]

Now we know that we can be saved from our sins, and that the kingdoms of this world will submit to your great kingdom.

"Glory to God in the highest heaven, and on earth peace to those on whom his favor rests."[‡]

Amen.

---

[*] Luke 2:30-32

[†] John 1:14

[‡] Luke 2:14

For Lent, Leading Up to Easter

Lord,

In the days leading up to Easter we want to contemplate and understand more fully the suffering death of the Lord Jesus whereby we are forgiven and his glorious resurrection whereby we are empowered to live.

This great mission to heal a broken world was your plan. Jesus gave up his life; it was not taken from him. In his death on the cross death itself was defeated. The power of sin was broken. The intent of the Evil One was thwarted.

We need these days to meditate on this great saving act.

Please focus our attention.

Release us from our trivial concerns.

Protect us from distractions.

Embolden us in the face of dangers.

Lessen our talk and increase our listening.

Captivate our minds.

Tame our hearts.

Increase our longing to know you.

For we "want to know Christ—yes, to know the power of his resurrection and participation in his sufferings, becoming like him in his death, and so, somehow, attaining to the resurrection from the dead."*

In Christ's name. Amen.

---

* Philippians 3:10-11

For Easter, Resurrection Day

Almighty God,

On this day we rejoice in the glory of resurrection.

The tomb is empty.

Death could not hold the Lord Jesus. His body saw no decay. His enemies did not win. The earth could not contain him.

We are emboldened by the power of resurrection.

We are encouraged by the hope of resurrection.

We are enlightened by the truth of resurrection.

So help us, dear God, to have a daily expectation that we will encounter the living Lord Jesus wherever we live.

Help us to live in submission.

And empower us to bring this message of resurrection into every dark and desperate corner of this world.

In the name of the resurrected Lord Jesus.

Amen.

Part 8

PRAYERS FROM SCRIPTURE

Prime Prayer: The Lord's Prayer

Our Father in heaven,
hallowed be your name,
your kingdom come,
your will be done,
    on earth as it is in heaven.
Give us today our daily bread.
And forgive us our debts,
    as we also have forgiven our debtors.
And lead us not into temptation,
but deliver us from the evil one.

Matthew 6:9-13

Prayer for the Abundant Life

And this is my prayer: that your love may abound more and more in knowledge and depth of insight, so that you may be able to discern what is best and may be pure and blameless for the day of Christ, filled with the fruit of righteousness that comes through Jesus Christ—to the glory and praise of God.

Philippians 1:9-11

114

Longing for God

You, God, are my God,
*   earnestly I seek you;*
I thirst for you,
*   my whole being longs for you,*
in a dry and parched land
*   where there is no water.*
I have seen you in the sanctuary
*   and beheld your power and your glory.*
Because your love is better than life,
*   my lips will glorify you.*
I will praise you as long as I live,
*   and in your name I will lift up my hands.*
I will be fully satisfied as with the richest of foods;
*   with singing lips my mouth will praise you.*

Psalm 63:1-5

Prayer of Confession

Have mercy on me, O God,
*   according to your unfailing love;*
according to your great compassion
*   blot out my transgressions.*
Wash away all my iniquity
*   and cleanse me from my sin.*
For I know my transgressions,
*   and my sin is always before me.*
Cleanse me with hyssop, and I will be clean;
*   wash me, and I will be whiter than snow.*
Let me hear joy and gladness;
*   let the bones you have crushed rejoice.*
Hide your face from my sins
*   and blot out all my iniquity.*
Create in me a pure heart, O God,
*   and renew a steadfast spirit within me.*
Do not cast me from your presence
*   or take your Holy Spirit from me.*
Restore to me the joy of your salvation
*   and grant me a willing spirit, to sustain me.*

Psalm 51:1-3, 7-12

Prayer for Strength, Love, and the Fullness of God

For this reason I kneel before the Father, from whom every family in heaven and on earth derives its name. I pray that out of his glorious riches he may strengthen you with power through his Spirit in your inner being, so that Christ may dwell in your hearts through faith. And I pray that you, being rooted and established in love, may have power, together with all the Lord's holy people, to grasp how wide and long and high and deep is the love of Christ, and to know this love that surpasses knowledge—that you may be filled to the measure of all the fullness of God.

Now to him who is able to do immeasurably more than all we ask or imagine, according to his power that is at work within us, to him be glory in the church and in Christ Jesus throughout all generations, for ever and ever! Amen.

Ephesians 3:14-21

—Part 9—

ONE-SENTENCE PRAYERS

Some of the most powerful prayers are voiced in a single sentence.

"God, have mercy on me, a sinner" (Luke 18:13). Jesus said a despised tax collector praying that prayer went home justified, in contrast to a Pharisee using high and mighty (and self-righteous) words in his prayer. Prayer is not for show.

It is good for us to have some one-sentence prayers that we have memorized that we can pray easily, quickly, and in response to changing circumstances throughout the day. Here are some suggested prayers. You may want to choose 10 to commit to memory.

One-sentence prayers for daily patterns

• Thank you for this new day and a fresh start.

• As I lay down to go to sleep, let me rest in the knowledge of your goodness and love.

• Grant me patience, dear Lord.

- Protect my children today, Lord, and let them see you in every choice they make.

- Your blessings are abundant, dear Lord, and so we thank you for this meal.

- Help me to forgive, dear God, as you have forgiven me.

- I submit myself to you, gracious Lord.

- Help me to be patient and forbear other people today, dear God.

- As I read your word now, dear God, open my eyes to the depth of your truth.

One-sentence prayers for special help

- My heart is broken right now, O God.

- Grant me wisdom, God, for this important decision.

- Help me to hold on.

- I am fearful today, O God. I need your peace.

- Help me to make the decision that will honor you.

One-sentence prayers of praise and thanksgiving

- Thank you, Lord, for the beauty of your creation.

- I praise you, God, whatever this day may bring.

- Thank you for saving me, Lord God.

- I praise you, O God, because your goodness never changes.

- Prepare my heart to worship you now, O God, in spirit and in truth.

One-sentence prayers for those in need

- Please heal this person who needs your healing—mind, heart, and body.

- Help me to see this person as you do.

- Give me compassion for the poor, dear God.

Two- and three-word prayers

- Rescue me.

- I confess.

- Protect me.

- Thank you.

- Glory to God!

- Have mercy.

- Forgive me.

- I love you.

- I praise you.

- Help _____.

- Protect my kids.

My own prayer:

Do you ever wish you understood the Bible better?

Almost everyone does. Mature believers and new believers. Young and old. Those who have read the Bible for years and those just starting out.

How to Understand the Bible: A Simple Guide, will help you gain an overall perspective on the flow and meaning of Scripture. It addresses questions like: What is the big picture of the Bible? What about Bible translations? How should we understand the stories of the Old Testament? How should we interpret what the prophets had to say? How should we understand the teachings of Jesus? What was Jesus teaching in the parables? How can we hear God's voice in Scripture? What are the proper ways to apply Scripture to life today?

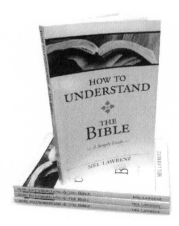

More resources at:

www.PrayersForOurLives.org

- Printable prayers. As a bonus for purchasing this book, "printable prayers" are downloadable PDFs you can print and display as you wish. Where prompted, use password.

password: 7373

- Church resources, including: pastors' guide, bulletin inserts, prayer campaign plan, bulk order information, etc.

- Audio prayers.

- Gift ideas.

- Prayer teachings.

- and more to come.

Made in the USA
Columbia, SC
09 March 2018